A Little Book of
Sensual Comfort

. . .

Also by Jennifer Louden:

The Woman's Comfort Book

The Couple's Comfort Book

And forthcoming:

The Pregnancy Comfort Book

A
Little
Book
· · · of · · ·

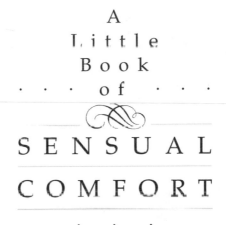

SENSUAL

COMFORT

· · ·

Jennifer Louden

HarperSanFrancisco
A Division of HarperCollins*Publishers*

Library of Congress Cataloging-in-Publication Data

Louden, Jennifer.
    A little book of sensual comfort / Jennifer Louden.—
1st ed.
        p.   cm.
    ISBN 0–06–251112–2 (pbk.)
    1. Conduct of life.   2. Human comfort.   3. Sensuality.
I. Title.
BJ1491.L68   1994   93–46348
155.9'11—dc20   CIP

        96 97 98 ❖ HAD 10 9 8 7 6 5 4

This edition is printed on acid-free paper that meets the American National Standards Institute Z39.48 Standard.

*W*hen you think of comfort, what do you think of? Name some of the things you find comforting. Right now, just make a quick list in your head. Now consider: how many of these items involve bodily pleasure?

When I think of comfort, I think of laying my head against my partner's chest, feeling completely safe and at peace. I taste cold milk and warm chocolate chip cookies melting on my tongue on a crisp fall day. I feel myself snuggling into a fluffy sweater, then digging in the warm dirt, planting scratchy spring bulbs. Comfort is the memory of skinny-dipping in a cold Florida spring on a scorching summer day or the caress of flannel sheets along my body as I stretch out for a good night's sleep. Comfort is tender sex, back tickles, foot rubs, toast and tea, the eucalyptus scented air of a Northern California forest, the voice of my best friend on the phone.

Comfort has many meanings and facets for each person. There is spiritual nourishment, and emotional sustenance. There are comforts for moments of solitude, and the comfort that comes from being listened to by someone you love. But perhaps the most potent, and universal, face of comfort is the physical. Soothing our animal self, meeting our most basic needs, reassuring our skin, our muscles, our bones, our bodies that we are snug, warm, peaceful, and taken care of as well as healthy, vital, joyful, and *alive*.

But we live in an age where sensual comfort is not particularly celebrated or given much attention. Pleasure has gotten a dubious name, thanks in part to the over-the-top style of the past decade. But how our souls crave sensorial solace! Whether it be the firm touch of a massage or the release of endorphins that come with a belly laugh, we *do* have bodies, and those bodies need to be taken care of, need to be pleasured. I suspect some of us would like simply to be giant heads: logical, cerebral, efficient, not against having a little fun, but hey, let's not get too carried away. Then there are those folks who resemble cats, purring with pure satisfaction when stroked, or putting their entire concentration into batting around a ball. It is the knowledge, the style, that these cat people (or dog people if you prefer) possess that this book seeks to imitate, seeks to reacquaint you with.

Let these simple ideas, some of which can be done by yourself, and some of which are most effective with a partner, inspire you to comfort yourself in an unabashedly tactile, luxurious, voluptuous, nonsensical, throw-caution-to-the-wind way. Let yourself go, even if just for a moment, and encounter a pleasure or two that will wipe away stress, clear your mind, and satisfy your cravings. Treat yourself to a taste of truly sensual comfort.

Relax

Lie down someplace quiet. Close your eyes. Take a deep breath. Hold it for a moment. Slowly let it out. Inhale. Imagine you are breathing pure relaxation in. Hold your breath. Now exhale, and imagine you are breathing out all the tension of your day, your week, your life. Do this a few more times.

Mentally, scan your body. Are there areas of tension? Inhale and send your breath of pure relaxation to the tense area. Imagine your breath curling around the knotted muscle, the stored stress. Exhale sharply, expelling every bit of tension from this area. Do this with all the other tense areas in your body. Take all the time you need. Now, imagine someone is giving you a gentle massage. The hands touching you are full of love. You are now filled with a deep and wonderful inner calm, and you are ready for whatever you want to do next.

Whenever you see the word *Relax*, refer back to these directions or relax in any way that feels good to you.

Beginning the Day with Comfort

Serve yourself morning coffee or hot tea in a nice cup. Linger over it in bed or in a patch of sunlight.

Play a piece of music you love. If your selection is one side of a cassette, tell yourself the world is not going to end if you take twenty minutes to sit still and relax.

Go for a brief early morning walk.

Spend ten minutes holding, talking, and just existing with the person you share your life with. Make this a priority in your daily life, no matter how busy.

You can do this if you're alone. Take a few moments to imagine your day going beautifully. Snuggle down in your warm sheets and hug yourself. Stretch like a cat. Repeat a few times to yourself, "This is going to be a great day."

Greet the sunrise. Don't move until it gets completely light.

Eat something natural and raw, like a ripe apple or a luscious strawberry. Concentrate on the taste, the texture, the aliveness of what you are eating. Let its energy course into your body.

Childlike Comfort

Light a sparkler and carve your name in the air.

Curl up with a blanket and watch the rain.

Listen to a children's choir.

Go for a walk in the moonlight.

Visit a children's bookstore. Considerably comforting places in their own right, they are filled with a wide selection of tantalizing titles. Look at the exquisite illustrations, inhale the clean smell of crisp, new pages.

You may be surprised by how familiar your bookseller will be with the sight of an adult searching for a long-forgotten title. Don't be ashamed to ask for help.

Relax Like an Animal

Lie down on the floor beside your animal friend, pretend a beloved pet is lying beside you, or picture a wild animal relaxing in her natural habitat.

Close your eyes and *Relax*. Feel yourself becoming your animal. Go inside its skin. You are now as free, as calm, as in-the-moment as this animal naturally is.

When you are ready, open your eyes and imitate your animal. How is he or she lying? Sprawled out, totally tranquil? Imitate this total abandon. Is your cat prowling around the room, jumping at shadows and breezes? Do this. Scratch, purr, stretch out in the sun. Perhaps you are imagining an otter gliding gracefully downriver? Feel the cool water sliding past you. Imagine what it feels like to be that playful, supple, and curious. Imitate the growls and yowls. Animals don't have jobs, deadlines, or bills. Allow yourself to feel happy and carefree. Let yourself go.

When you feel you've been animal-like long enough, collapse on the floor, close your eyes, and bask in your feelings of natural peace. If appropriate, hug your pet.

Meditation on Loving Yourself

Close your eyes and *Relax*. Focus on your breathing. Realize that each breath you take is irreplaceable, a one-time-only event. Breathe in and out a few times and let this fact sink in. Now, hold your hands. With your eyes still closed, caress and explore your hands. Absorb the fact that this is the only pair of hands like these in the universe.

Nowhere else does this pair of hands exist. Let your hands touch your opposite wrists and forearms. Stroke your skin and muscle. Allow your hands to travel up to your biceps and shoulders. Breathing deeply, hug yourself. Focus on your breath again. Like your breath, each moment of your life is unique and precious. Say to yourself or aloud, "I grant myself the right to exist and flourish. I am worthwhile."

When you are ready, take one more deep, deep breath, sending your conviction of self-worth throughout your entire body, and open your eyes.

Comfort Days

Have you ever packed a picnic, a nice picnic, just for yourself?

Take a day off to name and contemplate your passions. Write a bliss list.

My bliss list includes:

Gardening, Fortnum and Mason tea, sushi, rainy days in bed reading, chocolate, *Stuart Little* by E. B. White, Big Sur, a fall day in the New Hampshire woods, my best friend Barbra, living in Santa Barbara, women's rights, white water canoeing, and my honey, Christopher.

Drive to a nearby town or a strange part of your city that you have always wanted to explore. Spend the day being a tourist. Visit a bookstore, drink a cup of tea in a cafe. Let yourself be a stranger. Immerse yourself in a different culture. Get a glimpse of life outside your territory. Open yourself to that feeling of newness, of being someplace different.

Arrange your life so you don't have to speak for a day. Afterward, record your experiences and insights in your journal. Perhaps being without words will liberate you to hear your inner needs and wants more clearly.

Sensual Fun

Play with soap bubbles. Watch shadows dance on the wall. Play jacks. Finger paint and get real messy. Color in a coloring book.

Play in the rain. Play with a garden hose. Play tag with lawn sprinklers. Play with water in the bathtub or ocean. Slide in the mud. Make mud pies. Dribble water on paper and then trace the design with markers. Have a squirt gun fight with a friend.

Absorb the quiet of snow falling at night. Suck on a peppermint or squash a caramel in your mouth. Put on crazy music and move. Make sounds using your nose as a musical instrument.

Hug a dog. Hug a tree. Hug someone you love, really hard.

Skip. Jump rope. Turn a somersault. Throw a Frisbee. Roller-skate on a sidewalk. Roll down a grassy hill.

Shoot Silly String at your mate when he or she is taking life too seriously or not laughing at your jokes. Shoot Silly String at yourself when you nag about your partner's or child's faults.

Buy two squirt guns and squirt each other when you discover you are arguing about a stale issue.

Make a plaster hand print. Find a friend and draw each other's silhouettes. Have a food fight with marshmallows. Watch fireworks light up the sky.

Dig in the dirt. Press flowers. Go for a long walk in wet grass in your bare feet. Make mud pies. Make a sand castle, then smash it.

Bake cookies and eat them warm, with cold milk.

Physical Fun with Your Partner

Play "I can top that," a game created by author and therapist Dr. Harville Hendrix for his workshops. Stand facing each other. One partner goes first, doing something slightly crazy like jumping up and down on one foot. The second person jumps up and down on one foot *plus* pats himself on the head. Back to the first partner, who jumps up and down on one foot, pats herself on the head, *and* makes a bellowing noise. Keep taking turns adding elements until it is either physically impossible or you are laughing too hard to continue.

Drive out to the country or beach on a full moon and have a lunar picnic. Bring a Frisbee that glows in the dark.

Rent a horse and buggy and go for a ride in the moonlight, the snow, or a soft, spring rain.

Go skinny-dipping in a pool, ocean, pond, or quarry. Feel the balance between holding yourself up and the water supporting you.

Swim as close to each other as you can without touching.

Visit a playground in the moonlight. Swing on the swings and swish down the slide.

With a partner, lie under the covers with a flashlight and read a book together while eating Oreos. Choose something fun like a ghost story, fairy tale, or for the very silly or very tired, Dr. Suess (*Horton Hears a Who* is the best).

Climb a tree and sit on a branch. Ride bikes in the summer twilight. Rake leaves and jump in the piles. Lie outside and watch for falling stars, or make pictures from clouds as they go by. Go fishing and read poetry to each other while you wait. Walk in the wet grass barefoot holding hands. Jump on your bed and yell. Jump rope with your kids. Play Smashball in the living room.

Walk barefoot in an ocean, lake, fountain, or puddle together. Breathe together, or describe the sensations you are experiencing, or simply be in silence.

Run in a spring rain together. Jump in puddles. Squish mud between your fingers.

Locate a "you-pick-'em" field of strawberries or an apple orchard, pick a peck, and then make a pie together, or feed each other. Naked.

Hands in the Dirt

Nurture your green needs by visiting a particularly glorious florist shop. Linger over the flowers, sniff them, ask their names. Buy a single exquisite flower.

Collect a few small glass bottles and arrange unusual blossoms in them. Keep a bottle on your desk, and when the day is going badly, stop and study the flower for a moment.

Sketch or do a watercolor (not for art but for yourself) of a poppy, a palm tree, a white rose.

Check out a few garden picture books from the library, sip fruit juice, and imagine yourself surrounded by fragrant flowers.

This is easy and a great antidote for the winter blues. It sounds difficult, but once you try it, you'll do it every winter! Buy hyacinths, daffodils, narcissuses, crocuses, or tulips in October. Store for two months in the crisper of your refrigerator. In January, place bulbs in a pot or dish with pebbles, marbles, or rocks around them. (These just keep the bulb in place.) Water until the bulbs are almost covered. Place in a sunny (but not direct sun) location. Replenish the water every few days. They will bloom quickly and for a month or more.

Plant a garden to symbolize your relationship. It can be as simple as a few spring bulbs in a planter or as elaborate as the careful selection of plants whose names conjure up connections to your relationship or whose fragrances remind you of cherished memories. Tend your garden together to experience how nurturing your relationship connects you with life.

Surprise your partner by planting a few bulbs in a corner of a public park in honor of your love. Visit them daily while they bloom.

Find a peaceful garden or terrace spot outside your home to retreat to. Spend time here in silence, and try to carry that silence with you, to refer back to when you are angry with someone you love or burnt out on life.

Reconnect with the Earth

Next time you feel rotten, sluggish, or out of kilter, go to a place in nature you find inspiring. Find a place to lie down, directly on the ground. *Relax.* Close your eyes. Feel the stillness of the Earth under you. Feel its steady pulse.

Imagine the Earth is taking away your pain, sorrow, frustration, disappointments. Visualize these negative emotions and experiences leaving you and traveling down, down to the center of the Earth. See the molten core there. Imagine your feelings colliding with the pulsating, boiling, alive center of the Earth. Sparks fly, explosions sound. Out of the liquefied center beams a ray of healing energy. You watch this energy streaming up, up through the strata of rock and fossils, past tree roots and rabbits curled in their burrows, until this energy reaches you. It radiates up from the ground and through the soles of your feet. Breathe in this primeval life force. Feel the Earth's vitality as it travels up your calves and thighs, courses through your buttocks and into your womb, it fills your stomach and lungs, expands your heart, flows through each arm and lights up every one of your fingers. Up, up into your jaw and forehead. . . . And finally this pure energy illuminates your mind. You bask in this complete, wonderful, renewing warmth. This energy nourishes and feeds your entire being.

Now imagine the Earth's life force flowing out of your fingertips and toes, circling around and washing over you, then returning to the Earth. You are now part of the cycle of nature. Feel the steady, gentle pulse as this life force flows throughout your body, out your fingers and toes, and back down into the Earth. You are one with all of nature, you are connected to all that is alive.

Be part of this energy circle as long as you like. When you are completely at peace, filled with calm well-being, take one more deep, deep breath, creating a well of energy in your heart to draw from in the coming weeks. Thank the Earth. Know that you are forever part of the Earth and can return here for sustenance anytime you wish.

Winter Comfort

Curl up in flannel sheets with someone you love, be they human or animal.

Sip hot tea and watch the rain.

Make a snow angel.

Have a snowball fight, then run indoors and sip hot, mulled wine or apple cider by a roaring fire.

Roast marshmallows in a fireplace.

Spring Comfort

Walk around your neighborhood and look for new growth: buds, bulbs, grass shoots.

Plant herbs in a pot of dirt on a window sill.

Pin lilacs in your hair.

Investigate a mud puddle like a naturalist.

Plant daffodils, tulips, paper-white narcissus, and Easter lilies.

Plant a tree.

Climb a tree.

Have a tea party outdoors. Sip herbal tea and enjoy nature budding around you.

Summer Comfort

Fill a plastic wading pool with water and splash in it.

Eat ice cream while walking down a hot sidewalk. Let it drip all over your hands and face.

Make love under the stars.

Eat watermelon on a back porch. Have a seed-spitting contest.

Watch a thunderstorm from someplace safe.

Make Popsicles.

Camp out in the backyard with your best friend. Tell ghost stories. Wake up at three and sneak back into your bed.

Eat breakfast outside with the sun on your face.

Fall Comfort

Run through a tall cornfield.

Let the wind push you down the side-walk.

Fly a kite.

Go for a hayride.

Cook s'mores over an open fire.

Walk briskly and sniff the fall air.

Pop corn.

Howl at the moon.

Touch

Explore nature with your fingers, hands, cheeks, feet. You can do this alone or with a friend, taking turns blindfolding and guiding each other. A garden is bursting with unbelievable textures and feelings. Tickle yourself with the feathery lightness of a fern. Rub a smooth river rock against your palm. Caress a furry geranium leaf. Walk across the scratchy warmth of a concrete patio. Hold a struggling fish.

Wash your face slowly with a textured washcloth and warm water.

Caress yourself with a large feather. Great before bed.

Make a fist and run your knuckles over your arms and chest.

Roll a tennis ball under your bare feet.

Fill a basin with marbles and roll different parts of your body over them.

Take a day to explore every texture you can. Choose a silk shirt to wear, pay attention to the feel of your makeup. Become an explorer of textures.

With friends, sit in a circle all facing one direction and massage each other's backs. Concentrate on the caring that is uniting all of you. After awhile, turn around and massage the person who was massaging you.

After a meal, give your friend a hand massage.

Wash your lover's hair outside in the sunshine.

Tickle a friend's arm.

Sensory Delights with a Partner

Separately, select some objects with different textures: a peeled orange, silk shirt, feathers, ice cubes, eggs. Decide who will go first. Blindfold your partner and take turns putting items into hands or under feet, against elbows or behind knees. You can get as involved (and messy) as you wish. Each item should be thoroughly explored! Have your partner guess what he or she is feeling. You can write down answers and compare notes later. If you wish, make it into a game, where the person with the most correct guesses wins. (The prize is up to you.)

You can do the same exercise with your nose, consciously smelling fresh flowers, herbs, peeled and cut fruit, soap, perfume, bath gel, earth, new books. The sensorial options are endless.

Eat a meal blindfolded using only your hands. Don't eat the way you usually do. Chew longer, roll each morsel along the roof of your mouth, allow the essence of the food to flow into you. Stop often and breathe deeply. Stop and give each other a hand massage. Feed each other.

Try sampling different wines blindfolded. Or chocolates. Or ice creams. Or breads. Or . . .

Visit a sculpture garden. Take turns blindfolding each other and running your hands over different works of art. (Make sure this is okay with the guards; it usually isn't a problem with outdoor gardens.)

Finger paint together, blindfolded. Put down plastic or do it outside. Or do it blind-folded, outside, and naked! Watercolor together on the same piece of paper. Mold play-doh or clay together. Feel your fingers slipping over one another, your creative minds working together, without purpose, delighting in the sensations.

Touch Your Partner

Try nonsexual touching with your sexual partner. Decide on an equal period of time for both of you (twenty or thirty minutes apiece is great). Take turns touching each other any way you want except sexually (no genitals) and without conversation.

Arrange to have a massage together, lying side by side. Visit a day spa or have two massage therapists come to your home!

Use a different kind of touch with each other than you usually do. For example, if you always hug, shake hands or touch elbows or rub noses. If you always kiss each other on the lips, kiss each other on the hands or neck.

Self-Massage

Rub your hands together rapidly until they feel warm. Place your hands on your face. Hold them for a few seconds. Place two fingers from each hand in the center of your forehead. Rub in a circular motion toward and around your temples. Slide the heels of your palms to the tops of your cheekbones. Rub them in a circular motion downward over your cheeks, out toward your ears, and over your jawbones.

Move your hands to your head. Place your fingers near the back of your head and your thumbs behind your ears. Bring your thumbs and fingers together. Move slowly forward and then back, massaging your scalp. Gently grasp your hair and move the skin of the scalp in different directions. Tap your fingers vigorously over your scalp. Now bring your fingers down to the middle of the back of your neck. Rub in a circular motion.

Stretch your head gently to the right. With your fingers together, firmly run them up your neck muscles, to your ear. Switch and repeat.

Take a moment to study your hand. Lightly follow the vein structure. Pull each finger, twisting slightly. Squeeze and pull the fleshy part between your thumb and first finger. Push your knuckles into the palm. Don't forget the other hand.

Rub your back with a back brush, sponge, or back scratcher. Try lying on the floor and rolling your back over a ball. Different sizes reach different muscles. Experiment with a small child's ball, a tetherball, and a volleyball. See which feels best.

Massage your lower back by placing your thumbs in the small of your back. Move your thumbs and fingers together, grabbing and kneading the flesh.

Lying down, put one knee up and cross the other leg over it. Add oil to your hands, then rub them briskly together. Wrap your hands around your foot. Now, squeeze and pull the fleshy part between your toes. Knead the ball of your foot. Stroke the top and bottom of your foot lightly. Make a fist with your hand and push hard into the arch.

Sexual Comfort

Close your eyes and recall a sexual experience in which you felt secure, sexy, and loved. Enter into your wonderful memory as fully as possible. Feel all the sensations in your body. Now rub your hands together rapidly. Imagine that you are filling them with divine energy and love. Lay your hands on your stomach or neck. Feel the warmth and energy. Touch yourself with your electric fingers. Lightly run your fingers up and down your body. You deserve pleasure.

Stay with your memory of your good loving time while your hands slide over your stomach and through your pubic hair.

Flutter your fingers over your nipples. Tease yourself; don't be in a hurry. Now, drop a little oil onto your fingers. Run your hands quickly up and down your body. Experiment with different strokes. Let yourself go!

Sensual Fun with a Partner

Rent a video with a favorite love scene. Watch it, then reenact it together. (This may take some preparation. Don't be afraid to decorate a set, gather a few props, even costumes. . . .)

Have you ever taken your partner someplace blindfolded?

Play a favorite game. Naked.

Play strip gin rummy.

Dress up in each other's clothes—even underwear!

Trade with a friend: while you're out with your partner doing something boring, like buying new underwear at K-Mart, your friend sneaks into the house and arranges a romantic dinner in front of the fireplace; a bottle of champagne and a bubble bath with a trail of Hershey kisses leading the way from the front door to the bathroom; or flowers, dancing music, and a table full of delectable desserts, all of which can be smeared on one or more parts of the body. . . . Reciprocate when the time comes!

Sensual Artistry

With your partner, reserve an hour to be alone in a private space. Choose art materials you can use your hands with; clay or finger paints work well. Set up an inviting environment, one that will allow you to be comfortable naked *and* work with messy materials. An old sheet on your bedroom floor is one possibility.

Sit facing each other, naked or partially clothed, however you feel most comfortable. Study each other, taking one aspect of the body into your attention at a time. Start with the head and face, and work your way down. Touch your partner. Use different parts of your hand: little finger, palm, knuckle. Pay attention to how your partner's skin and bones feel under your hand. Sink into the magnificence and godliness of this body. Pay attention to the details: the back of the neck, the curve of a shoulder, the belly button.

When you have spent *a lot* of time treasuring the unique wonder of your lover's body, turn to your materials. Move very slowly. Immerse your hands in the paint or clay. Rub it between your fingers. Contemplate how many times these same hands have touched your partner. Close your eyes. Lose yourself in the sensuous textures of your materials. Let your hands explore viscerally and nonintellectually the link between the materials and your lover's body. Don't think about making anything on the paper or with your clay, just experience. When you feel finished, you are.

Rekindle Sensuality with Your Partner

Sit facing each other in a comfortable position. Close your eyes and *Relax*. . . . Continue to breathe slowly and deeply. In your own time and in your own way, imagine your heart. Visualize a flame or ball of light in your heart. It may be clear or it may be a color. Spend a moment enjoying the warmth, the power of the light. . . . Now imagine you are breathing into this light. With each of your powerful breaths, the light grows brighter and brighter, gradually filling your chest. . . . With another deep breath, the light begins to radiate up into your neck and face and head, filling your mind with a wonderful sense of balance and peace. . . . Continue to breathe deeply as you visualize this glowing illumination spreading along each of your arms. . . . The light now moves down, warming your stomach and genitals. . . . Another breath sends the warmth shooting down into your legs, all the way to your toes. . . . Take several more breaths to send this tingling, wonderful light throughout your body. . . . Bask in the sense of aliveness and well-being you've created.

And now, open your eyes and *without speaking*, hold hands and look into your partner's eyes. Keep taking deep breaths, focusing on the warm, beautiful light that is filling your body. Feel the light beginning to expand beyond you . . . out through your eyes and into the eyes of your beloved. With each breath you take together, the light grows stronger, connecting your hearts. Stay with this for a moment or two. Don't worry if you feel embarrassed or overwhelmed. Just keep breathing.

Maintaining eye contact and heart contact, let your mind drift back, back to when you and your lover first fell in love, a time when passion and fascination filled your life. Reach back into your memory and allow these beautiful memories to flow through you. Keep taking deep breaths. Keep feeling the love that fills you and fills your partner while you spend a few moments reliving the details of your shared past. What did your lover smell like? Do you remember a particular smile or gesture that captivated you? How did you feel? Where were you? Allow these powerful desires to arise.

Slowly, realize this isn't a memory but the present. This is actually happening. The person facing you is still the person you fell in love with. Allow this thought to break your defenses down just a little bit. Allow more of your love and admiration to flow. If you feel afraid or anxious, breathe into that fear and remember your partner is supporting you with her light, his love. Surrender to your feelings little by little. Trust your partner to stay with you. Breathe away your fears, breathe away your blocks, breathe away your anger. Allow yourself to open to your feelings. If you feel sexually aroused, let these feelings fill your heart and body too.

When you are ready, embrace your partner.

Wild Love

Find a very private spot in nature where you can make love without being disturbed or feeling self-conscious. It can be your own backyard or a hillside covered with wildflowers. The place must reassure the shiest person. Create a bed on which you can recline naked and be comfortable. The instructions below are intended as general guidelines, not a step-by-step visualization. Improvise!

Lie down next to each other on your backs and spend a few moments breathing deeply. Experience the air on your skin. Work on just being. What does it feel like to be outdoors and naked? Explore, silently, how the Earth feels under you. Imagine the ground supporting you, cradling you.

Visualize a golden cord running from the bottom of your heels deep into the Earth.

Take a moment to feel the energy running up from the Earth, along this cord, and into your body. This is healing, dynamic energy you are receiving through your golden cord. After a moment, hold hands. Now feel the energy running between you. Breathe deeply. Focus on creating a live connection with your partner. Taking lots of time, caress each other, imagining you are spreading this wonderful Earth energy all over your lover's body. When you begin to make love, concentrate on feeling the energy moving back and forth between you, and up and down between each of you and the Earth, connecting the rhythm of nature with the rhythm of your love. Imagine as you climax that you are sending healing, loving energy back into the Earth, the flowers, the trees, and also showering it around you, into the air, covering everything with a soft, shining coating of love.

Sexual Fantasies

In detail, write a sexual fantasy that you would like to have fulfilled by your lover. Sometimes, partners don't fantasize about each other. If that is the case, take one of your favorite fantasies and insert your partner. If you feel too embarrassed to dream, complete the sentence "A sexual fantasy I would like to act out with you is . . . " Trade your fantasies and surprise your partner by fulfilling her fantasy one day.

Simmering Sexual Feelings

Starting in the morning, roll over and caress your mate while whispering in his or her ear, "I want to make love to you tonight like lions mating on the veld." (Or something similar to that.) Don't squelch this by saying, "But tonight's the PTA meeting." If tonight isn't a good time for you, then lick your lover's ear and gently propose an alternative date. *Stick to that date!*

Throughout your day, massage your anticipation. Make whispered illicit phone calls about what you are going to do to each other that night; have lingerie, silk boxer shorts, scented massage oil, or a canister of whipped cream delivered to work with a naughty note; meet for lunch and pretend you are illicit lovers. Your imagination is the only limit. Spend the day simmering your excitement. Read erotica on your lunch hour, pleasure yourself while the kids are napping, or on the commute home fantasize about a fantastic sexual encounter you and your partner shared in the past. Once together in the evening, keep building the tension. Rub against each other "accidentally" while you're cooking dinner, go out to dinner and feed each other, take a shower together, take time to arrange the atmosphere in your bedroom, and then, finally, time for love. (Yes, you can do this with children. Five minutes of sexual innuendo over dessert while the kids watch TV, ten minutes of foreplay while the kids are in the bath, fifteen minutes of in-

tercourse after the kids fall asleep. Be creative; it doesn't have to be one continuous
encounter!)

Getting in the Mood

The sandwich press: The lighter partner lies
on top of the heavier, stretching out and
matching arm to arm, leg to leg. Turn your
heads to the side and lie cheek to cheek.
Breathe deeply. The person on the bottom
imagines himself or herself sinking into the
mattress or floor, while the person on top
concentrates on melting into the lover.

The brain press: Place your right hand
behind your partner's head at the base of the

skull, and your left hand over the forehead. Press firmly and hold for a count of twenty. Both of you breathe deeply, with your eyes closed, and concentrate on letting go of tension and worries.

Back body sweep: One partner sits with back straight and arms relaxed at the sides. The other partner stands behind and places one hand on each shoulder, about an inch away from the skin (you don't actually touch). Sweep the hands toward the opposite buttock, crossing midback. You are making an X across your partner's back. Move quickly. Repeat three times.

Whole body sweep: One partner lies down, eyes closed, arms and legs slightly apart, breathing deeply. To relax: The partner giving the sweep starts at the hands and sweeps up the arms and down the side of the body to the toes, again with hands one inch away from the body. Repeat two more times, then do the same sweep on the other side of the body. To revitalize: Sweep from the toe to the hand along each side of the body three times.

Standing sweep: Stand toe to toe, hips close together. Both persons place their hands on either side of the base of the other's spine (right above the buttocks). Press deeply, then run your fingers all the way up to your partner's neck, pressing firmly on the muscles on either side of the spine. Return your hands to the base of the spine and repeat two more times.

Ask and Ye Might Receive

One person becomes the receiver and one becomes the giver. The receiver's role is to relax and try to experience as much sexual gratification and arousal as he or she is capable of while giving explicit instructions to the giver. The giver concentrates on being as artistic and lavish a lover as he or she can be.

As receiver, gather any aids you would like the giver to choose from: massage oil, aromatherapy oils, feathers, or a vibrator (or two). Get comfortable, taking a few deep breaths. Tell the giver where to start on your body and what to do. For example, "Please start by lightly tickling my entire body with your fingertips, but avoid my breasts and

genitals until I tell you. . . . That's perfect.
I'm going to breathe and enjoy this for a few
moments. . . . Now massage my feet using
the massage oil. . . .You can touch me a little
harder. . . . Great." Keep giving instructions,
as specific as possible. Offer encouragement,
but be very clear in your own mind that this
is your time to receive exactly what you want.
Don't worry about the other person's needs.

As the giver, follow the receiver's instructions as explicitly as possible. Concentrate on staying relaxed by breathing deeply
and checking in with your own body. How
does it feel to be giving without receiving
anything back? Breathe into any feelings of
tension or performance anxiety. If you feel
unsure about an instruction, do it and then

ask, "Was that okay?" or "Did that feel good or would this feel better?" You can add your own creative touches, but primarily focus your energy on trying to fulfill your partner's requests.

When you are finished, talk about what this was like for each of you. End by reaffirming the date and time when the giver will become the receiver. Above all, stick to this appointment!

Sensing Your Partner

Suck your lover's fingers and toes. Toes have more nerve endings than genitals. Dip digits in hot fudge, fruit juice, or whatever other fluids appeal to your taste, and lick them clean.

Dribble water across a stomach and then blow gently.

Surprise your partner by decorating the bedroom. You could fill the room with balloons or flowers or light candles, play wild, tribal music, burn musky incense, and cover the bed with a fake animal throw.

Write down three brief, erotic fantasies, put them in a hat, and have your partner pick one to enact.

Take a walk in the woods and gather flowers to later adorn your partner's genitals with.

Sex in the kitchen adds new luster to the room faster then a remodeling job. Feed each other mango. Hold ice in your mouth while sucking parts of your lover's body. The kitchen table might be just the right height to lie back on while the other person stands or kneels. . . .

Blindfold your partner and make love while whispering everything you find attractive, arousing, and beautiful about him or her.

Body Delights

Focus on how you feel during an activity. As you walk, take turns concentrating on what your hands feel like, then your legs, then your neck, and so on. Feel your body coil and uncoil as you spring on a minitramp. Listen to your breath as you swim. Listen to the sound of the tennis ball hitting your racket. Let yourself enjoy the moment.

Dance at dawn to reggae music while you watch the sun rise. Boogie naked in the moonlight to big band tunes. Feel the music.

Get a massage. As the masseuse manipulates your body, concentrate on accepting the attention. Breathe away your nervousness at having someone touch you. Close your eyes and imagine the masseuse sending you healing energy. Direct this energy to where you are tense or sore. Allow yourself to be the center of attention. Take and don't worry about giving anything back. You deserve all this attention. You are worth it.

Dress in flowing clothing. Play wild music. Throw your arms and hands out. Stand on the toes of one foot and push off with the other in a counterclockwise movement. Keep pushing, moving faster and faster. Let your cares and worries fly away from you.

Bathing Pleasures

Prepare your bathroom for bathing. Light your candles. Place a flower or plant near the water.

Start with a brief, warm shower. Using a loofah or bathing brush with a shower gel or soft soap, scrub your body. Rinse off in cool water.

Towel off briskly and slip into a soft, clean robe.

Fill your clean tub with hot water. Add the scent of the day. Consider floating flowers on the water.

While your tub is filling, sit quietly. Concentrate on your breathing.

Step outside the bathroom and announce, "I am leaving the world out here." Close the door firmly behind you.

Start your music now.

Think positive things about your body as you slip into the water.

Study a candle flame. Trace the edge of a leaf. Contemplate the color of a flower. Meditate. Do a deep stretch. Play with the water. Rub yourself all over with a square of silk.

Touch and pleasure yourself. Play with bath toys. Just be in the primordial warmth of your bath.

When you are finished, pull the drain, stand up, and recite, "Everything negative in my life is now washing down the drain."

Shower in the Dark

Showering in the dark is a wonderful way to relieve sensory overload. Imagine this as a way to wipe your mind clean.

This shower works best in total darkness. If you are afraid of falling, add a candle or use a night-light.

Concentrate solely on the sensual plea-
sures of the water. Shut out everything else.

Small Baths

Fill a basin with warm water. Add chamo-
mile tea to the water for a soothing effect or a
teaspoon of cayenne pepper for rejuvena-
tion. Play some upbeat music. Slip your feet
into the water. Sip wine or herbal tea. *Relax.*
Thank your feet for supporting you. Let
your body's energy replenish itself.

Soak your hands in the hot water. Add a
drop of rosemary or sage essential oil. Massage your hands and rotate your wrists while

you soak. Also try soaking your hands in warmed olive oil.

Waterfall Visualization

Imagine yourself in a lush tropical rain forest. All around you, exotic birds make magical music. Soft, warm sunlight flickers through tall trees. There is a stream near your feet. You follow the stream until it leads you to a tranquil pool. At the far edge of the pool is a gentle waterfall, surrounded by a balmy mist.

You slip out of what you are wearing and step into the pool. The water is the perfect temperature. You wade until you are directly under the waterfall.

Relaxing totally, you let the water wash over you. It washes away all your tensions, all your worries, all your gloomy feelings. This is a magical waterfall, and it fills you with a wonderful feeling of well-being. It nurtures every cell in your body until you tingle all over. Stay here as long as you need, washing away all your stress, all your anxiety.

Whenever you are ready, you slip back to shore and into your clothes. Finally, you gently float back to consciousness.

Open your eyes and bask in your feeling of well-being and buoyant energy.

Shower with Your Mate

Initiate a shower together. Wash your lover. All over.

Serve your partner a surprise snack in the shower or tub. Sections of orange to suck on while she showers, cookies and coffee while he soaks, a glass of champagne for both of you and after a sip you jump in the tub with your lover, fully dressed. . . . (Okay, maybe not fully dressed.)

Couples' Baths

For a wild and tropical shared bath, add one 10-ounce can of unsweetened coconut milk,

10 drops gardenia oil, and 10 drops of oil of amber to warm water. Hang wind chimes at the open window, slice pineapple and mangoes to eat while in the tub, and imagine yourselves in a tropical jungle.

Slide into this bath on a hot summer day or night. Two hours or more before bathing, place 2 drops of peppermint oil in enough water to make a tray of ice cubes. (You might want to make two or three trays.) Freeze. Prepare cool drinks, like hard apple cider with lemon twists, iced cappuccino, or tall frosty mugs of beer. Run hot water and drop in 15 drops of magnolia oil, 10 drops of orange blossom oil, and 2 drops of peppermint oil. Put your drinks and the ice cubes by the side of the tub. Lie in the tub until you are hot enough to melt, then pick up ice cubes and slowly run them over each other's bodies.

Have you ever considered taking a bath together—in the morning? What a way to start the day. Bathe with eucalyptus soap and a tub filled with 5 drops of eucalyptus oil, 10 drops bergamot, 10 drops lavender, and 3 drops of cinnamon. Lean back, sip your morning coffee, and listen to NPR together.

Another morning bath idea is designed to help with hangovers you might have gotten wining and dining each other the night before. Try 5 drops of grapefruit oil, 3 drops rosemary, 2 drops fennel, and 1 drop juniper in a warm, not hot, bath.

Forgiving Waters

Decide on a time on or near the full moon when you can privately visit a body of water or a swimming pool. You can also do this as a visualization, without water.

Begin by focusing on your breath. Feel how easily it glides in and out of your body. Imagine your breath moving throughout your body, easing every area of tension it encounters. Breathing deeply, walk slowly toward the water. Stop to gaze up at the moon. Feel the calm energy of the moonlight finding its way deep into your soul. The moonlight and your slow, deep breaths mingle and relax your body completely.

You reach the water. The moonlight gives the water magical powers tonight. Disrobe and slip in. Cup your hands together, fill them with water, and pour the water on yourself. With each touch of the magic water, say, "I forgive myself." "I forgive myself for (fill in what you need to forgive yourself for: hurting someone you love, a mistake, regrets). I am now releasing my remorse and sorrow. I forgive myself."

After you have forgiven yourself for everything you can, visualize someone who has hurt you. Splash water at this image, saying, "I forgive you." Imagine others who have hurt you. Release them by anointing their images with water too.

When you are finished, glide underwater. As the magic water closes over your head, say to yourself, "I am now cleansed. I am free."

Walk out of the water and dress. Take a moment to gaze at the moon and to be thankful for your new peace. Breathing deeply, return the way you came.

A Reconnecting Ritual for Couples

Lie together in bed, spoon fashion. The partner on the inside is the receiver and is enfolded in the arms of the partner on the outside, who is the giver.

Close your eyes and *Relax*. Focus on your breathing. After a few moments, become aware of your partner's breathing. When the receiver is ready, he or she inhales deeply, holds the breath for a moment, then exhales. The giver matches this breathing pattern. Inhale, hold, and exhale together for several minutes. During this, the receiver concentrates on receiving the energy of his or her partner's breath and the giver concentrates on sending energy by emphasizing his or her exhalations.

When the receiver is ready, he or she begins to vary the breath so that as the giver breathes out, the receiver breathes in. One partner holds a breath in, while the other blows a breath out. Continue for several minutes.

When the receiver is ready, he or she turns to face the giver. Gaze into each other's faces. Bask in the connection silently.

Peace Meditation

Close your eyes. Inhale and exhale gently. Focus on your breath going in, coming out. Now focus your closed eyes on the center of your forehead. Don't strain. Remember to breathe. Inhaling and exhaling, repeat silently to yourself, "I am at the center of peace. All is well in my world." Repeat this again and again while breathing deeply and maintaining your awareness on your forehead area.

Relax the Senses with Your Mate

Take turns. One person lies down, eyes closed, and *Relaxes* while the other person kneels or sits beside. Do this in silence, no music. The person sitting speaks softly, "Relax, eyes, relax. Forget about seeing. For the next few minutes, you don't have to focus, you can relax. Relax, eyes, let go. . . . Relax, nose, relax. Forget about smelling. For the next few minutes you don't have to smell anything. You can relax. Relax, nose, relax, you can let go. . . ." Repeat with mouth (forget about tasting), hands (forget about touching), and ears (forget about hearing). Finally, end by saying, "And now, you are floating, totally relaxed. And when you return, whenever you're ready, your senses will be completely clear, open, and sharp like never before." Speak rhythmically and very slowly, lulling your partner into relaxation. Repeat when ready with the other person.

Sweet Scents

Schedule an hour or two to stock up on your familiar smells. Fill your house, work, and car with emergency smell stashes. A sample vial of Chanel No. 5 might rest in your glove compartment for a soothing sniff during a traffic jam. Try cooking for smell when you are down. If an aroma can't be stocked, go after that scent when you need comfort. Take a walk and sniff for newly mown grass, wood smoke, or dinner cooking.

Put a drop of your favorite scent in your vacuum cleaner bag.

Put two drops of your favorite essential oil in a shallow bowl of warm water.

Dampen a tissue with two or three drops of ylang-ylang, patchouli, geranium, linden blossom, or rose, then wrap this tissue in a piece of cloth and tuck in with your clothes.

(Don't put the oil directly on your clothes, because some oils stain.)

Tuck sachets in your car, briefcase, desk, or between your sheets.

Hang a small cotton bag of lavender from your rearview mirror and experience more calming drives.

Immersed in Music

Choose flowing, healing music. Lie down with your feet near your speakers. Support your neck with a pillow. Imagine the music is water flowing around you, lifting you up, washing away all your tension. Let the music cradle you, enfold you, caress you.

When you are completely relaxed, allow the music to enter through the soles of your feet. Feel the music filling your feet. Allow it to move through your ankles, calves, thighs. Feel the vibrations inside you. Allow the music to flow up your pelvis, into your stomach, lungs, out along your arms, tingling through each and every finger. Now feel the music filling your heart. Finally, the music courses through your neck and face, massaging each muscle, filling every fiber of your head with beauty and relaxation.

Silent Solitude

Breathe slowly. Concentrate on the small moment of silence that exists between your inhalation and exhalation. If you are distracted by noises, focus on the silence between the noises. Imagine the silence underneath the ocean. Let this sense of immense solitude fill you. Stay with this as long as you like, then focus on the sounds around you again. Slowly open your eyes.

This is a great exercise to do in nature, high on a hill with the wind blowing through your hair, off in a corner of a garden, or by a body of water.

Ending the Day with Comfort

Before bedtime, select something special to wear. Consider sipping some herbal tea or enjoying a relaxing bath.

Light a candle or two by your bed. Turn off the other lights. Stretch across your bed, taking your time, exaggerating your movements. Feel the cool sheets against your body. Moving slowly, open a book of poetry (or an uplifting or thought-provoking book) and slowly read a page. Allow the wisdom and beauty of what you are reading to enter your mind. Put the book aside. Take a minute to concentrate on the candle flame. Blow out the candle and curl into peaceful sleep.

For a Comforting Sleep Pillow

Try mixing 2 ounces rose petals, 1 ounce mint, 1 ounce rosemary, and a tissue with a few drops of clove oil on it. Stuff into a muslin bag, then tuck or sew into a pillow. Rest on this pillow whenever you have trouble sleeping.

Another calming mixture can be made from 2 ounces agrimony, 1 ounce woodruff, 1 ounce crushed cloves, 1 ounce crushed and dried orange peel, 1 ounce orris root powder, and 2 drops orange oil.

To help you remember your dreams, tuck 8 ounces of mugwort into your pillow.

Sleep in the Moonlight

A magical event! Try sleeping in the moonlight on your roof, in your backyard, in the middle of the desert, or on top of a mountain. Plan a trip with several close friends to camp out under a full moon. Make sure you bring a warm sleeping bag and an insulating mat.

Lie on your back and watch the moon rise. Watch the stars, any clouds, the blackness around everything. Close your eyes and compare the darkness around you with the darkness inside. Feel the vastness of space. Imagine the moon is bathing you in magical radiance. Perhaps you want to sing a song to the moon or dance a moonlight jig.

Sleep Rituals for Couples

Read something beautiful to each other before bed. Try Wendell Berry's or Emily Dickinson's poetry. Visit a bookstore together to find a book that appeals to both of you.

Try sitting back to back and breathing deeply for one minute.

Look into each other's eyes, take a deep breath, and repeat, silently or aloud:

Breathing in, I welcome sleep,

Breathing out, I let go.

*Jennifer Louden leads workshops
and comfort seminars across the country.
She lives in Los Angeles with her husband,
Chris and their dog, Atticus.*